Starting a Business in the Philippines

(An Easy Guide for Foreigners)

by Michelle D Martinez

Introduction

The Philippines is strategically located in the Asia-Pacific region which is the intersection of international shipping and airlines. The Philippine economy has been growing and expanding in the last couple of years due to the influx of foreign investors and businesses.

There are several reasons why foreign investors prefer to invest and build their business operations in the Philippines. First, Filipinos are literate, highly educated and competent labour force being the third largest speaking nation in the world. Second, research shows that labour costs in the Philippines are less than one fifth in comparison with the United States. Thus business process outsourcing, call centres and information technology services can save up to 50% business costs. Third, the Philippine Government has identified special economic zones that offer PEZA registered companies 100% percent exemption from corporate income tax and thereafter 5% special tax on gross income and exemption from national and local taxes among other tax incentives. Fourth, the Philippine Retirement Authority offers different visa options for foreign investors and retirees making it easier to live in the Philippines. Fifth, the Filipinos are known for their hospitable warm friendly nature and with more than 7,000 islands to explore there is so much to do and to see in the Philippines.

This handbook will give you basic knowledge and information of business structures and business activities available for foreign nationals and foreign companies. You will learn the basic company set up and different business structure including the benefits and incentives of investing and operating in Special Economic Zones and produce a plan that works best for you and your business.

Legal Disclaimer
Copyright @ 2020 Michelle D Martinez
All rights reserved.

The contents of this handbook are summaries and compilations of selected issuances from various government agencies available as of the date of writing and is intended to provide general information and not legal advice and should not be regarded as such. While care and consideration was used in the creation of this handbook, they do not cover exhaustively the subjects it treats but is intended to answer important and broad questions.

The author does not guarantee and accepts no legal liability, for the accuracy, reliability, currency or completeness of any material on this booklet or any mentioned websites. Your use and implementation of any suggestions set out in this handbook and mentioned websites does not create any lawyer-client relationship between you and the author. This booklet is intended for guidance only and formal legal advice should be sought in particular matters. You should seek appropriate independent legal advice before making any decisions based on materials found on this booklet or any mentioned websites.

For my late father Fructuoso, who inspired me to be a lawyer
and
my mother Porfiria, who taught me about selfless love.

Table of Contents

Chapter I - Business structures
1. Domestic corporations
    1.1. Sole proprietorship
    1.2. Partnership
    1.3. Corporation
        - Stock
        - Non-stock
    1.4. One Person Company
2. Foreign Corporations
    2.1. Resident foreign corporation
        - Branch of a foreign company
        - Regional operation headquarters
        - Regional headquarters
        - Representative branch
    2.2. Non-resident foreign corporation

Chapter II - Business activities
1. List A Foreign ownership is limited by mandate of the Constitution and specific laws
    1.1. No foreign equity
    1.2. Up to 25% foreign equity
    1.3. Up to 30% foreign equity
    1.4. Up to 40% foreign equity
2. List B Foreign ownership is limited for reasons of security, defence, risk to health and morals and protection of small and medium scale enterprises
    2.1. Up to 40% foreign equity

Chapter III - Philippine Visa
1. Special Investors visa under the Board of Investments
    1.1. Special Investor's Resident visa (SIRV)

1.2. Special visa for employment generation (SVEG)
2. Special Resident Retiree visa under the Philippine Retirement Authority
   1.1. Special Resident Retirees Visa (SRRV) Smile
   1.2. Special Resident Retirees Visa Classic
   1.3. Special Resident Retirees Visa Human Touch
   1.4. Special Retiree Resident Visa Courtesy
   1.5. Special Retiree Resident Visa Extended Courtesy
3. Work visa under the Philippine Immigration Act 1940
   3.1. Pre-arranged employee commercial visa (9G)
   3.2. Pre-arranged employee non-commercial visa (9G missionary visa)
   3.3. Special non-immigrant visa or section 47(a)(2) of the Philippine Immigration Act 1940
   3.4. Special non-immigrant multiple entry visa under Executive Order 226 as amended by Republic Act 8756 (RQHQ)

Chapter IV - Basic taxation
1. Tax consequences on corporation
2. Tax consequences on employees

Chapter V - Board of Investments (Executive Order 226)
   The Special Economic Zone Act of 1995
    (Republic Act 7916)
   Philippine Investment Promotion Plan

List of abbreviations

The abbreviated words refer to the following:

ACR	-	Alien Certificate of Registration
AEP	-	Alien Employment Permit
ADLE	-	Additional Deduction for Labour Expense
BIR	-	Bureau of Internal Revenue
BOI	-	Board of Investments
BP	-	Batas Pambansa
BPO	-	Business Process Outsourcing
OIC	-	Omnibus Investments Code
DBP	-	Department of Bank of the Philippines
DENR	-	Department of Environment and Natural Resources
DME	-	Domestic Market Enterprise
DND	-	Department of National Defence
DOJ	-	Department of Justice
DOLE	-	Department of Labor and Employment
DTI	-	**Department of Trade and Industry**
ECC	-	Emigration Clearance Certificate
EO	-	Executive Order
FIA	-	Foreign Investments Act
GOCC	-	Government Owned and Controlled Corporations
HDMF	-	Home Development Mutual Fund
IC	-	Identification Card
IPP	-	Investment Priorities Plan
IT	-	Information Technology
ITH	-	Income Tax Holiday
LDA	-	Less Developed Area
MCIT	-	Minimum Corporate Income Tax
NBI	-	National Bureau of Investigation

NICA	-	National Intelligence Coordinating Agency
OPC	-	One Person Company
PAGCOR	-	Philippine Amusement and Gaming Corporation
PEZA	-	Philippine Economic Zone Authority
PhilHealth	-	Philippine Health Insurance Corporation
PHSF	-	Personal History Statement Form
PIPP	-	Philippine Investment Promotion Plan
PNP	-	Philippine National Police
PRA	-	Philippine Retirement Authority
PRC	-	Professional Regulation Commission
PWP	-	Provisional Work Permit
RA	-	Republic Act
RDO	-	Regional District Office
RHQ	-	Regional or Area Headquarters
ROHQ	-	Regional Operation Headquarters
RW	-	Regional Warehouse
R & D	-	Research and Development
SBMA	-	Subic Bay Metropolitan Authority
SEC	-	Securities and Exchange Commission
SIRV	-	Special Investors Visa
SRC	-	Special Return Certificate
SRRV	-	Special Resident Retirees Visa
SSS	-	Social Security System
SVEG	-	Special Visa for Employment Generation
TEZ	-	Tourism Enterprise Zone
TRAIN	-	Tax Reform for Acceleration and Inclusion
VAT	-	Value Added Tax

Chapter I
Business structures

Chapter I
Business Structures

There are two kinds of business structures in the Philippines, domestic company and foreign company. This chapter will discuss the basic features of these types of business structures and and the requirements and procedures to set up your own business.

Question: Can a foreign national engage in business in the Philippines?
Answer: Yes. There are several ways you can establish, own, operate and manage a business in the Philippines. You need to know the business structures and the advantages and disadvantages of each and choose one that best suits your needs.

Question: What are the types of business structures available?
Answer: There are two kinds
1. Domestic company
2. Foreign company

Domestic company

Question: What are the types of domestic company?
Answer: The types of domestic business structures are
1. Sole proprietorship
2. Partnership
3. Company
4. One Person company

B. Foreign corporations

Question: What are the types of foreign company in the Philippines?
Answer: There are two kinds:
1. resident foreign corporation with a branch, office or sales in the Philippines
2. non resident corporation who derives income from but has no presence in the Philippines

Question: How can a foreign company engage in business in the Philippines?
Answer: A foreign corporation can engage as
1. domestic corporation with 100% foreign equity; or as a
2. resident foreign corporation

Question: What are the types of resident foreign corporation?
Answer: There are 4 different types
1. Branch of a foreign company
2. Regional operation headquarters
3. Regional or area headquarters
4. Representative branch

Domestic Company

Sole Proprietorship

Question: What are the features of single proprietorship?
Answer: The single proprietor
1. is the simplest form of business structure and relatively easy to put up thru DTI
2. is allowed for foreign national subject to the restrictions and limitations by the Philippine Constitution and special laws
3. is liable for all your business losses and your business creditors can go after your personal assets and vice versa your creditors for your personal liabilities can go after your business assets.

Question: What are the requirements and procedure to register a single proprietorship?
Answer: To register a single proprietorship you must do the following steps with different government agencies
1. Department of Trade and Industry (DTI)
1.1. Go to https://bnrs.dti.gov.ph/ and complete online application form
1.2. Pay the registration fees
1.3. After your DTI Certificate of Registration is released proceed the next step

2. Barangay
2.1. Fill-up barangay application form where your office is located
2.2. Submit application form together with DTI Certificate of Business Registration, 2 valid identifications (ACR for foreign nationals), proof of address (contract of lease)
2.3. Pay the registration fees
2.4. After your Barangay Clearance Certificate is released proceed to the next step

3. Mayor's Office
3.1. Fill up application form at City or Municipality where your office is located
3.2. Submit application form together with DTI Certificate of Registration, Barangay Clearance Certificate, 2 valid identifications (ACR for foreign nationals) and proof of address
3.3. Pay the registration fees
3.4. After your Mayor's business permit and licence is released proceed to the next step

4. Bureau of Internal Revenue
4.1. Fill up BIR Form 1901 Application for Registration for sole proprietorship at the Regional District Office (RDO) where your business is located
4.2. Submit form together with DTI Certificate of Registration, Barangay clearance, Mayor's business permit, proof of address, valid identifications (ACR for foreign nationals)
4.3. Pay the registration fees
4.4. Register your book of accounts and receipts/invoices
4.5. After the release of your Certificate of Registration (BIR Form 2303) you can now begin to operate your business.

Partnership

Question: What are the features of a partnership?
Answer: A partnership
1. is formed when individuals pool their resources and funds to engage in a common business objective

2. each one of the partners acts as manager and agent of the partnership and an act of one of the partners bind the partnership
3. your liability as a partner are unlimited similar to a single proprietorship and creditors may ask payment for some or all of partnership debts
4. is required to register an Article of Partnership with the SEC. The law governing partnerships are Articles 1767 to 1867 of the Civil Code
5. the change in the composition of the partnership such as death of a partner dissolves the partnership.

Question: What are the steps to register a partnership?
Answer: To register a partnership you must do the following steps with different government agencies:

1. Securities and Exchange Commission (SEC)
1.1. Go to http://www.sec.gov.ph/online-services/ and complete online application form
1.2. Pay the registration fees
1.3. After your SEC Certificate of Registration is released proceed to the next step

2. Barangay
2.1. Fill-up barangay application form where your office is located
2.2. Submit application form together with SEC Certificate of Business Registration, 2 valid identifications (ACR for foreign nationals), proof of address (i.e. contract of lease)
2.3. Pay the registration fees
2.4. After your Barangay Clearance Certificate is released proceed to the next step.

3. Mayor's Office
3.1. Fill up application form at City or Municipality where your office is located
3.2. Submit application form together with SEC Certificate of Registration, Barangay Clearance Certificate, 2 valid identifications (ACR for foreign nationals) and proof of address
3.3. Pay the registration fee

3.4. After your Mayor's business permit and licence is released proceed to the next step

4. Bureau of Internal Revenue
4.1. Fill up BIR Form 1903 Application for Registration for partnership at the RDO where your business is located
4.2. Submit form together with SEC Certificate of Registration, Barangay clearance, Mayor's business permit, proof of address, valid identifications (ACR for foreign nationals)
4.3. Pay the registration fees
4.4. Register your book of accounts and receipts/invoices
4.5. After the release of your Certificate of Registration (BIR Form 2303) you may begin to operate your business.

Corporation

Question: What are the features of a corporation?
Answer: A corporation
1. is the preferred type of business structure because it is treated as a separate legal entity with the same rights as an individual
2. can own properties, incur debts and has the right to sue and be sued.

Question: What are the classes of corporations?
Answer: There are two kinds
1. stock is when capital stocks are divided into shares and profits are authorised to be distributed
2. non-stock is not for profit

Question: What are the requirements for the incorporation/formation stage?
Answer: To incorporate a company
1. there must be at least 5 incorporators but not more than 15 who are
1.1. natural persons
1.2. of legal age and
1.3. majority are residents of the Philippines

2. An incorporator must subscribe to at least one share of stock. A corporation cannot be an incorporator; however, a corporation can be a stockholder after it is incorporated.

3. Twenty-five (25%) percent of the authorised capital stock must be subscribed and twenty-five (25%) percent of the subscribed capital stock must be paid at the time of incorporation which amount should not be less than PhP5,000.00.

4. The Articles of Incorporation, By-Laws, Treasurer's Affidavit, Bank Certificate must be submitted and registration fee paid at the Securities and Exchange Commission.

Question: What are the management features of a corporation?
Answer: The features are:
1. the incorporators are usually the company's board of directors
2. the board of director must:
2.1. own at least one share of capital stock; and
2.2. majority are residents of the Philippines.

Question: Who are the required officers in a corporation?
Answer: The corporate officers are
1. President who must be a member of the board of directors
2. Secretary who must be a resident and citizen of the Philippines
3. Treasurer
4. Other officers can be created under the by-laws

Note: The President cannot be the Secretary or Treasurer at the same time.

Question: What are the steps to form a corporation?
Answer: To register a company you must do the following steps with different government agencies:

1. Securities and Exchange Commission (SEC)
1.1. Go to http://www.sec.gov.ph/online-services/ and complete online application form
1.2. Pay the registration fees

1.3. After your SEC Certificate of Registration is released proceed to the next step

2. Barangay
2.1. Fill-up barangay application form where your office is located
2.2. Submit application form together with SEC Certificate of Business Registration, 2 valid identifications (ACR for foreign nationals), proof of address (i.e. contract of lease)
2.3. Pay the registration fees
2.4. After your Barangay Clearance Certificate is released proceed to the next step

3. Mayor's Office
3.1. Fill up application form at City or Municipality where your office is located
3.2. Submit application form together with SEC Certificate of Registration, Barangay Clearance Certificate, 2 valid identifications (ACR for foreign nationals) and proof of address
3.3. Pay the registration fees
3.4. After your Mayor's business permit and licence is released proceed to the next step

4. Bureau of Internal Revenue
4.1. Fill up BIR Form 1903 Application form for corporation at the RDO where your business is located
4.2. Submit form together with SEC Certificate of Registration, Barangay clearance, Mayor's business permit, proof of address, valid identifications (ACR for foreign nationals)
4.3. Pay the registration fees
4.4. Register your book of accounts and receipts/invoices
4.5. After the release of your Certificate of Registration (BIR Form 2303) you may begin to operate your business.

One Person Company (OPC)

Question: What are the features of a OPC?
Answer: In a One Person Company:
1. a single stockholder is also the incorporator

2. you have full control and authority of the business
3. your liability is limited
4. you are the sole director and president
5. you are required to designate a nominee and an alternate nominee
6. the nominee or alternate nominee shall replace you in case of incapacity or death

Question: Who may form a OPC?
Answer: The following may form a OPC
1. Foreign nationals subject to limitations in law and locals
2. Trust being managed by a Trustee (not trust entity)
3. Estate

Question: Who are not allowed to form a OPC?
Answer: The following are not allowed to form a One Person Company
1. Natural person for the purpose of exercising a profession
2. Banks, financial institutions and quasi-banks
3. Pre-need, trust and Insurance companies
4. Public and Publicly-listed companies
5. Non-chartered government owned and/or controlled corporations

Question: What are the documents needed to set up an OPC?
Answer: The documents needed are:
1. name reservation form
2. cover sheet
3. Articles of incorporation
4. written consent of the nominee and alternate nominee
5. additional documents
5.1. Foreign Investments Act (FIA) form for foreign nationals
5.2. proof of authority to act on behalf of the trust or estate for trusts in case of Trust
5.3. affidavit of undertaking to change company name (as necessary)
5.4. Tax identification number

Question: What are the steps to register a OPC?
Answer: At present, the registration process is done manually with the SEC

1. Securities and Exchange Commission
1.1. Reserve company name
1.2. Submit the Articles of incorporation with the written consent of the nominee and alternate nominee
1.3. Payment of filing fees
1.4. After your SEC certificate of registration is released, proceed to the next step

2. Barangay
2.1. Fill-up barangay application form where your office is located
2.2. Submit application form together with SEC Certificate of Business Registration, 2 valid identifications (ACR for foreign nationals), proof of address (i.e. contract of lease)
2.3. Pay the registration fees
2.4. After your Barangay Clearance Certificate is released proceed to the next step

3. Mayor's Office
3.1. Fill up application form at City or Municipality where your office is located
3.2. Submit application form together with SEC Certificate of Registration, Barangay Clearance Certificate, 2 valid identifications (ACR for foreign nationals) and proof of address
3.3. Pay the registration fees
3.4. After your Mayor's business permit and licence is released proceed to the next step

4. Bureau of Internal Revenue
4.1. Fill up BIR Form 1903 Application for Registration for sole proprietorship at the Regional District Office (RDO) where your business is located
4.2. Submit form together with SEC Certificate of Registration, Barangay clearance, Mayor's business permit, proof of address, valid identifications (ACR for foreign nationals)
4.3. Pay the registration fees
4.4. Register your book of accounts and receipts/invoices
4.5. After the release of your Certificate of Registration (BIR Form 2303) you may begin to operate your business.

B. Foreign company

Resident Foreign Company

Branch Office

Question: What are the features of a branch of a foreign company?

Answer: The branch of a foreign company in the Philippines
1. is an extension of the parent company and can engage in business activities similar to home country
2. does not have a separate legal from parent company and formation, existence, dissolution including liabilities in the Philippines are considered of parent company
3. allowed to derive income and conduct business in same manner as parent company subject to conditions prescribed by Philippine laws and regulations
4. US$200,000 minimum capital is required, however US$100,000 capital is allowed provided
4.1. activities involve advance technology or
4.2. employs at least 50 employees;
5. US$200,000 required capitalization, if it will be a Domestic Market Enterprise (DME) and intends to only sell goods and services to Philippine market
6. US$100,000 required capitalization, if it will be an export-oriented enterprise that exports goods and services amounting to 60% or more of its gross sales.
7. has a resident agent in the Philippines.

Question: What are registration requirements for a Representative Office?

Answer: You are required to obtain a License to Do Business in the Philippines from SEC and submit:
1. SEC Application Form No F-103- Application of a Foreign Corporation to establish a Branch Office in the Philippines
2. Name verification slip
3. Certified copy of the Board Resolution of the parent company to open a representative office and naming a resident agent to

receive summons and legal proceedings who can either be a Philippine resident or a domestic corporation, in the absence the SEC may be served
4. Certified copies of the Articles of Incorporation of the parent company
5. Latest audited financial statements certified by an independent certified public accountant and authenticated by the Philippine embassy
6. Proof of inward remittance of US$200,000 or US$100,000 as initial capital
7. Resident agent acceptance of appointment
8. Endorsement or clearance from government agencies as applicable.

Question: What are the tax consequences of a branch of a foreign company?
Answer: The tax consequences are
1. taxed like a local corporation, 30% corporate income tax, 12% VAT and other taxes
2. repatriation of income is subject to 15% branch profit remittance tax unless reduced by applicable tax treaties between parent country
3. if branch office is located inside special economic zone of the Philippine Economic Zone Authority (PEZA), it is exempted from tax on branch profit remittance and can avail of other tax incentives.

Regional Operation Headquarters (ROHQ)

Question: What are the features of a regional operating headquarters (ROHQ)?
Answer: The regional headquarters
1. has subsidiaries, branches, affiliates or clients in the Asia-Pacific region and other foreign markets
2. does not have a separate legal from parent company and the formation, existence, dissolution including liabilities in the Philippines are considered of parent company
3. considered an extension of the parent company and allowed to derive income in the Philippines by qualifying services to its head

office, affiliates, subsidiaries or branches in the Asia-Pacific region and other foreign markets like:
- General administration and planning
- Business planning and coordination
- Sourcing/procurement of raw materials and components
- Corporate finance advisory services
- Marketing control and sales promotion
- Training and personnel management
- Logistics services
- Research and development services and product development
- Technical support and maintenance
- Data Processing and communication; and
- Business development

4. is not allowed to directly or indirectly solicit or market goods and services on behalf of parent company or affiliates.
5. US$200,000 capital is required
6. has a resident agent in the Philippines

Question: What are registration requirements for ROHQ's
Answer: You are required to obtain a License to Do Business in the Philippines from SEC and submit:
1. Name verification slip
2. Certification from Philippine Consulate/Embassy or the economic government agency of the parent company certifying that the company is engaged in international trade with subsidiaries, affiliates, branches in the Asia Pacific region
3. Certification from the principal officer authorising the registration
4. Proof of inward remittance of U$200,000 as initial capital
5. Registration data sheet
6. Latest financial statement
7. Endorsement from the Board of Investment
8. Endorsement from government agencies (as applicable).

Question: What are the tax consequences of a regional operation headquarters?
Answer: The tax consequences are

1. income tax rate of 10%
2. repatriation of income is subject to 15% branch profit remittance tax subject to applicable tax treaties between parent company
3. exempted from branch profit remittance if registered with PEZA)
4. managers and technical expatriates are taxed at 15% on gross income.

Regional Headquarters (RHQ)

Question: What are the features of a regional or area headquarters?
Answer: The regional or area headquarters
1. an administrative branch of the foreign company engaged in international trade in the Asia-Pacific region and other foreign markets
2. purpose is to supervise, inspect or coordinate its subsidiaries, branches and affiliates in the Asia-Pacific region.
3. does not have a separate legal from parent company and formation, existence, dissolution including liabilities in the Philippines are considered of parent company
4. can perform general administration, business planning and communication centre for subsidiaries
5. may source raw materials or market products, train employees or conduct research and development within Philippines under prescribed conditions
6. US$50,000 annual remittance is required to cover operating expenses and annual inward remittance to support operating expenses
7. not allowed to solicit or market goods and services
8. not allowed to manage any subsidiary or branch office
9. not allowed to earn income in the Philippines
10. used by multinational corporations to operate their business overseas in a cost effective manner using local labour and tax incentives.

Question: What are registration requirements for RHQ's
Answer: You are required to obtain a License to Do Business in the Philippines from SEC and submit:

1. Name verification slip
2. Certification from Philippine Consulate/Embassy or the economic government agency of the parent company certifying that the company is engaged in international trade with subsidiaries, affiliates, branches in the Asia Pacific region
3. Certification from the principal officer authorising the registration
4. Proof of inward remittance of U$50,000 as paid up capital and annual support for operating expenses
5. Registration data sheet
6. Latest financial statement
7. Endorsement from the Board of Investment
8. Endorsement from government agencies (as applicable).

Question: What are the tax consequences of a regional headquarters or regional operating headquarters?
Answer: The RHQ is exempted from paying income tax and VAT. It can avail of Tax incentives from the BOI. The managers and technical expatriates are taxed at 15% on Gross income.

Representative office

Question: What are the features of a representative office?
Answer: The representative office
1. acts as a local office and extension of the parent company
2. parent company subsidizes and liable for all operating expenses
3. is not allowed to earn income in the Philippines
4. deals directly with the clients of its parent company overseas
5. is fully funded by the parent company and at least US$30,000 annual inward remittance for operating expenses.
6. allowed the following activities:
    - facilitate orders of customers or clients from its head office
    - disseminate information and conduct promotional activities about the products of its head office
    - undertake quality control of products from its head office; and

- undertake other related administrative activities for its head office

Question: What are registration requirements for Representative Office

Answer: You are required to obtain a License to Do Business in the Philippines from SEC and submit:
1. SEC Application Form No F-104- Application of a Foreign Corporation to establish a Representative Office in the Philippines
2. Name verification slip
3. Certified copy of the Board Resolution of the parent company to open a representative office and naming a resident agent to receive summons and legal proceedings who can either be a Philippine resident or a foreign national residing in the Philippines
4. Certified copies of the Articles of Incorporation of the parent company
5. Latest audited financial statements certified by an independent certified public accountant and authenticated by the Philippine embassy
6. Proof of inward remittance of US$50,000 as initial capital
7. Resident agent acceptance of appointment
8. Affidavit executed by the President or resident agent that the foreign corporation is solvent and sound financial condition.

Question: What are the tax consequences of a representative office?

Answer: A representative branch can engage in business but cannot earn income, they are considered as non-resident foreign corporation and therefore exempted from income tax.

Question: What are the advantages of setting up a representative office?

Answer: It is an ideal business structure for foreign companies to reduce cost by operating their back office, administrative operations, customer service, marketing platform IT and technical support.

Other government agencies

Question: What are other government requirements to operate the business?

Answer: The Social Security Law (Republic Act No 8282) mandates that all employees including foreign nationals under 60 years old and earn more than 1,000 Philippine pesos are required to contribute to the:

1. Social Security System (SSS)

This government agency aims to provide private employees and their families protection against disability, sickness, retirement and death. The employers withhold from the employee's salary a monthly contribution (usually 4%) and the employer also contributes (usually 8%) in the fund.
For further information, go to https://www.sss.gov.ph/

2. Home Development Mutual Fund (HDMF also known as PAG-IBIG)

This is a mandatory savings system that provides housing loans to private and government employees and also those who are self-employed (optional). The monthly contributions are Ph. 200 pesos to be paid equally by employer and employee.
For further information, go to https://www.pagibigfund.gov.ph/

3. Philippine Health Insurance Corporation (PhilHealth)

This agency promotes health care by providing discount on medical expenses to employees. The monthly contributions are 2.75% of the employee's basic monthly salary to be paid equally by employer and employee.
For further information, go to https://www.philhealth.gov.ph/

4. Department of Environment and Natural Resources (DENR)

This agency is responsible for the protection and preservation of Philippine natural resources.
For further information, go to https://emb.gov.ph/

Foreign nationals employed in the Philippines must make contributions to SSS, HDMF and PhilHealth unless exempted under the Philippines Totalization Agreements.

Chapter II

Business activities

Chapter II
Business activities

The Foreign Investments Act of 1991 (FIA) regulate the participation of foreign nationals and promote foreign investments to develop and contribute to the Philippine economy. The Foreign Investment Negative List A limit the participation of foreigners in accordance with the Philippine Constitution and specific laws while Negative List B limit the participation of foreigners for security, defence, risk to health and morals or protection of small and medium sized businesses. However, over the years, the list has been updated and relaxed to keep up with the changing times. This chapter will enumerate the recently promulgated 11th Regular Foreign Investment Negative List A and B as at 29 October 2019.

Question: Are foreign nationals allowed to participate and engage in business in the Philippines?

Answer: Foreign nationals are allowed to own and invest as much as one hundred percent (100%) equity in areas not restricted by the Philippine Constitution and special laws like the Negative List under the Foreign Investments Act.

Question: What are the types of businesses activities not allowed for foreign national's in the Philippines?

Answer: The Negative List A and B are:

List A: Foreign ownership is limited by mandate of the Constitution and specific laws

No foreign equity

1. Mass media, except recording and internet business

Internet business refer to internet access providers that merely serve as carriers for transmitting messages rather than being the creator of messages/information (DOJ Opinion No 40 (s1998).

2. Practice of professions, including radiologic and x-ray technology, law, criminology, and marine deck officers and marine engine officers, subject to the Annex on Professions indicating professions where
2.1. foreigners are allowed to practice in the Philippines subject to reciprocity; and
2.2. where corporate practice is allowed

Foreign nationals may teach at higher education levels if subject being taught is not a professional subject (included in a government board or bar examination).

Practice of profession is an activity/undertaking rendered by a registered and licensed professional or a holder of a Special Temporary Permit as defined in the scope of practice of a professional regulatory law (Section 1(b) of Professional Regulation Commission (PRC) Resolution No 2012-668.

3. Retail trade enterprises with paid-up capital of less than US$2.5 million.

Full foreign participation is allowed for retail trade enterprises
a. with paid up capital of U$2,500,000 or more provided that investments for establishing a store is not less than U$830,000; or
b. specializing in high end or luxury products, provided that the paid up capital per store is not less than U$250,000.

4. Cooperatives

5. Organization and operation of private detective, watchmen or security guard agencies

6. Small-scale mining

7. Utilization of marine resources in archipelagic waters, territorial sea, and exclusive economic zone as well as small-scale utilization of natural resources in rivers, lakes, bays and

lagoons

8. Ownership, operation and management of cockpits

9. Manufacture, repair, stockpiling and/or distribution of nuclear weapons

10. Manufacture, repair, stockpiling and/or distribution of biological, chemical and radiological weapons and anti-personnel mines

11. Manufacture of firecrackers and other pyrotechnic devices

Up to 25% foreign equity

1. Private recruitment, whether for local or overseas employment

2. Contracts for the construction of defence-related structures

Up to 30% foreign equity

1. Advertising

Up to 40% foreign equity

1. Contracts for the construction and repair of locally-funded public work except:

1.1. Infrastructure/development projects covered in Republic Act (RA) No. 7718 and

1.2. Projects which are foreign-funded or assisted and required to undergo international competitive bidding.

For the construction stage of these infrastructure projects, the project proponent may obtain financing from foreign and/or domestic sources and/or engage the services of a foreign and/or Filipino contractor. Provided, that in case an infrastructure or development facilities operation requires a public utility franchise, the facility operator must be a Filipino or if a corporation, must be duly registered with the SEC and owned up to at least 60% by Filipinos. In the case of foreign contractors, Filipino labour shall be employed or hired in the different phases of the construction where Filipino skills are available (Section 2(a) of RA 7718)

2. Exploration, development and utilization of natural resources

Full foreign participation is allowed through financial or technical assistance agreements entered into with the President

3. Ownership of private lands

4. Operation of public utilities, except power generation and the supply of electricity to the contestable market and similar businesses or services not covered by the definition of public utilities

A public utility is a business or service engaged in regularly supplying the public with some commodity or service of consequence such as electricity, gas water, transportation, telephone or telegraph service

5. Educational institutions other than those established by religious groups and mission boards, for foreign diplomatic personnel and their dependents and other foreign temporary residents, or for short-term high-level skills development that do not form part of the formal education system as defined in Section 20 of Batas Pambansa (BP) No. 232 (1982)

6. Culture, production, milling, processing, trading except retailing, of rice and corn and acquiring, by barter, purchase or otherwise, rice and corn and the by-products thereof

Full foreign participation is allowed provided that within the 30-year period from start of operation, the foreign investor shall divest a minimum of 60% of their equity to Filipino citizens

7. Contracts for the supply of materials, goods and commodities to GOCC, company, agency or municipal corporation

A contract may be awarded to any contractor or bidder who is a citizen, corporation or association of a foreign country the laws or regulations of which grant similar rights and privileges to citizens of the Philippines.

8. Operation of deep sea commercial fishing vessels

9. Ownership of condominium units

10. Private radio communications network.

List B: Foreign ownership is limited for reasons of security, defence risk to health and morals and protection of small and medium scale enterprises

Up to 40% foreign equity

1. Manufacture, repair, storage and/or distribution of products and/or ingredients requiring Philippine National Police (PNP) clearance (subject to exemptions).

2. Manufacture, repair, storage and/or distribution of products requiring Department of National Defence (DND) clearance (subject to exemptions).

3. Manufacture and distribution of dangerous drugs.

4. Sauna and steam bathhouses, massage clinics and other like activities regulated by law because of risks posed to public health and morals, except wellness centres.

5. All forms of gambling except those covered by investment agreements with PAGCOR

6. Domestic market enterprises with paid-in equity capital of less than the equivalent of U$200,000.

7. Domestic market enterprises which involve advanced technology or employ at least 50 direct employees with paid-in equity of less than the equivalent of U$100,000.

Chapter III

Philippine Visa

Chapter III
Philippine Visa

Question: What types of visa can a foreign national have to work and live in the Philippines?

Answer: There are several visa options you can apply depending on your purpose and personal circumstances.

1. If you want to own and manage your own business you can apply for the Special Investors Visa options under the Board of Investments (BOI)
1.1. Special Investors Visa (SIRV) or
1.2. Special Visa for Employment Generation (SVEG)

2. If you want to live and retire in the Philippines you can apply for the Special Resident Retiree Visa Options under the Philippine Retirement Authority (PRA)
2.1. Special Resident Retirees Visa Smile (SRRV Smile)
2.2. Special Resident Retirees Visa Classic (SRRV Classic)
2.3. Special Resident Retirees Visa Human Touch (SRRV Human Touch)
2.4. Special Retiree Resident Visa Courtesy (SRRV Courtesy)
2.5. Special Retiree Resident Visa Extended Courtesy (SRRV Extended Courtesy)

3. If you have an employer, your visa options would depend on your employment arrangement with your employer i.e. 9G Visa.

Special Investors Visa thru Board of Investments

Question: What type of visa are available for foreign investors under the Board of Investments?

Answer: You have two options
1. Special Investor's Resident Visa (SIRV)
2. Special visa for employment generation (SVEG)

Special Investor's Resident Visa (SIRV)

The SIRV aims to attract foreign investments and require investors to remit and invest at least US$75,000 in listed economic activities Book V of the Omnibus Investments Code.

Question: What are the features of SIRV?
Answer: The Special Investor's Resident Visa
1.1. allows you to reside indefinitely in the Philippines with multiple entries
1.2. requires you to remit at least US$75,000 to Philippines to invest amount in economic activities listed in Book V of the Omnibus Investments Code (EO No 226, as amended)
1.3. remittance can be done thru accredited banks in the Philippines
1.4. you can include your spouse and unmarried children below 21 years of age.

Question: Who are qualified to apply for the SIRV?
Answer: To qualify for a SIRV you have to
1. be at least 21 years of age
2. not have been convicted of crime involving moral injustice
3. not afflicted with any dangerous or contagious disease
4. not have been institutionalised for any mental disorder or disability
5. be willing and able to invest at least US$75,000 which can be lowered to US$50,000
6. be a holder of a tourist visa with at least one-month validity.

Question: What kind or form of investments are allowed under the SIRV?
Answer: Your investment must be one of the following
1. Investments or shares of stocks in existing, new or proposed companies like:
1.1. Publicly-listed companies
1.2. companies engaged in the IPP of the BOI

1.3. manufacturing and services sectors; or companies whose activities fall in any of the following major sectoral classifications:
- a. business services (such as BPO, consultancy, etc.)
- b. communication services
- c. construction and related engineering services
- d. distribution services
- e. educational services
- f. environmental services
- g. financial services
- h. health related and social services
- i. tourism and travel related services
- j. recreational, cultural and sporting services
- k. transport services, and
- l. other services not included elsewhere.

1.4. government securities

2. Investments in condominium units or partnerships and ownership of stocks of wholesale trading are not allowed.

Note: A foreign investor who already made actual investment in business activities eligible under the SIRV program may be considered for evaluation towards his application

Question: What are the documents required for SIRV application?
Answer: The following documents are required (3 sets):
a. notarized application form with recent ID pictures
b. Personal History Statement form (PHSF) from National Intelligence Coordinating Agency (NICA)
c. Police clearance from foreign national's country or residence authenticated by Philippine Embassy or Certification of no criminal liability by the INTERPOL Division of the National Bureau of Investigation (NBI)
d. medical certificate from foreign national's home country certifying the applicant is physically fit validated by the

Bureau of Quarantine
e. certification from the Development Bank of the Philippines (DBP) in relation to the remitted amount
f. birth certificate authenticated by Philippine embassy
g. marriage certificate authenticated by Philippine embassy

Question: What is the use of the SIRV Card?
Answer: For purposes of travel, you can present the SIRV card in replacement of the Alien Certificate of Registration Card (ACR card) and be exempted from getting the:
1. Special Return Certificate (SRC) and
2. Emigration Clearance Certificate (ECC).

Special Visa for Employment Generation (SVEG)

The SVEG is a special visa for qualified non-immigrant foreigner who employ at least 10 Filipinos in a lawful and sustainable enterprise, trade or industry. As a SVEG holder you and your spouse and dependent children are considered special non-immigrants with multiple entry privileges and conditional extended stay without need of prior departure.

Question: What are the features of Special Visa for Employment Generation?
Answer: The conditions of SVEG are
1. you shall actually, directly or exclusively engage in a viable and sustainable commercial investment or business enterprise, exercise or perform management acts or has the authority to hire, promote and dismiss employees
2. you evidence a genuine intention to indefinitely remain in the Philippines
3. you shall employ at least 10 Filipinos in your business
4. you are not a risk to national Philippine security.

Question: What is the application process for SVEG?
Answer: The application process is
1. the Commissioner of Immigration shall receive and resolve your application within 5 days of filing and payment of fees
2. Once approved, the Commissioner shall issue a Notice of Approval and you will be required to report for registration and documentation at the Bureau of Immigration
3. you will be issued an Alien Certificate of Registration (ACR) and an Identification Card (IC) upon payment of fees.

Special Resident Retiree Visa (SRRV) thru Philippine Retirement Authority (PRA)

The SRRV is managed by the PRA to promote and grant those who would like to retire in the Philippines services, benefits and comfort to make their stay valuable and beneficial.

Question: What are the options for retirees who want to live in the Philippines?
Answer: The Philippine Retirement Authority initiated the Special Resident Retiree Visa Options for those who want to live and bring their family for business, investment, study, medical and retirement purposes in the Philippines.

Question: What are the benefits of Special Retiree Resident Visa?
Answer: The benefits are
1. you have multiple entry privileges and you may travel outside the Philippines and enter anytime
2. you may live work and study in the Philippines
3. you are exempted from
3.1. customs duties and taxes for personal and household goods worth US$7,00 for one-time importation availed within 90-day from issuance of the SRRV
3.2. Bureau of Immigration ACR I-Card
3.3. exit and re-entry permit of the Bureau of Immigration

3.4. annual registration requirement of the Bureau of Immigration
3.5. pensions remitted are tax-free
3.6. securing student visa if you want to study
3.7. travel tax if your stay in the Philippines is less than 1 year from the last entry date
4. free assistance in securing documents from other government agencies.

Question: What type of visa are available for retirees?
Answer: Retirees can avail of the following visas

1. Special Resident Retirees Visa (SRRV) Smile
Features:
1.1. you are at least 35 years old of good health
1.2. US$20,000 visa deposit for you and two dependents
1.3. additional deposit US$15,000 for more than two dependents
1.4. deposit stays in a PRA designated bank and cannot be used for investment
1. 5. deposit can be withdrawn after cancellation of visa.

2. Special Resident Retirees Visa Classic
Features:
2.1. if you are at least 35 up to 49 years old of good health you need to deposit US$50,000
2.2. if you are at least 50 years old without pension, you need to deposit US$20,000
2.3. if you are at least 50 years old with a minimum monthly pension of US$800 for single applicant and US$1,000, you need to deposit US$10,000.
2. 4. deposit is used for the purchase of condominium units or residential long term lease which are ready for use
2.5. additional deposit US$15,000 for more than two dependents.

3. Special Resident Retirees Visa Human Touch
Features:

3.1. you are at least 35 years of age with at least US$1.500 monthly pension

3.2. US$10,000 visa deposit for you and one dependent

3.3. deposit stays in a PRA designated bank and cannot be used for investment

3.4. deposit can be withdrawn after cancellation of visa

3.5. you need medical certificate of pre-existing condition requiring medical assistance

3.6. health insurance policy you can use in the Philippines.

4. Special Retiree Resident Visa Courtesy

Features

4.1. you are at least 50 years of age and above or 35 years and above who is a former Filipino citizen, or

4.2. you have served in the Philippines as diplomat, ambassador, officer/staff of international organizations

4.3. US$1,500 visa deposit

4.4. employment certificate from the international organization or agency or birth certificate for former Filipino citizen.

5. Special Retiree Resident Visa Extended Courtesy

Features:

5.1. you are 50 years of age and above

5.2. you can be a retired diplomatic, military, professor, scientists, philanthropists and other notable professions as described in PRA Circular No. 012 of 2013.

5.3. US$1,500 visa deposit which can be used to buy condominium or long term lease

5.4. additional US$1,500 per dependent visa deposit in excess of two

5.5. certificate of achievement issued by international body or organisation.

Work visa under Philippine Immigration Act 1940

Foreign nationals who are employed by a company or a business enterprise can apply for work visa thru their employers. The work visa would depend on the size and type of company you work for and your role in the company.

Question: What types of work visa are allowed for foreign nationals?
Answer: The 4 types of work visa are
1. Pre-arranged employee commercial visa (9(g))
2. Pre-arranged employee non-commercial visa (9(g)) (missionary visa)
3. Special Non-Immigrant Visa or 47 (a) (2) of the Philippine Immigration Act 1940
4. Special Non-Immigrant Multiple entry Visa under EO 226 as amended by RA 8756 (RQHQ).

Pre-arranged employee visa (9G visa)

Question: What are the features of a Pre-arranged employee commercial visa (9(g))
Answer: The features are
1. you can work and stay in the Philippines usually with the same period with your employment contract
2. you can enter and exit Philippines anytime
3. an Alien Employment Permit (AEP) issued by the DOLE is required
4. a Provisional Work Permit (PWP) can be issued and used while visa is on process
5. you must be in gainful employment with domestic or foreign company licensed to do business in Philippines
6. most commonly applied working visa.

Pre- arranged employee non-commercial visa (9G missionary visa)

Question: What are the features of a Pre-arranged employee non-commercial visa (9(g)) (missionary visa)

Answer: The features are

1. you can work and stay in the Philippines for one year and renewable
2. you can enter and exit Philippines
3. domestic company can serve as Petitioner of the visa application
4. you must be involved in the community immersion project in a community or assigned location engaging in missionary, social, rehabilitation or medical mission.
5. you must not receive or generate income from the domestic company.

Special Non-immigrant visa or Section 47(a)(2) of the Philippine Immigration Act 1940

Question: What are the features of a Special Non-Immigrant Visa or section 47 (a) (2) of the Philippine Immigration Act 1940

Answer: The features are

1. you can work and stay in the Philippines as a non-immigrant
2. for a temporary period under conditions the President may prescribe
3. you need employer sponsorship
4. visa is valid for the term of contract or one year whichever is shorter
5. the company is limited to employ foreign nationals to less than 5% of the total workforce
6. you are exempted from ACR I-card requirement
7. usually applied by investors or employees of PEZA and/or BOI registered companies or oil industries.

Special Non-Immigrant Multiple entry Visa under EO 226 as amended by RA 8756 (RQHQ)

Question: What are the features of Special Non-Immigrant Multiple entry Visa under EO 226 as amended by RA 8756 (RQHQ)

Answer: The features are

1. you are an executive of a regional or area headquarters of multinational companies
2. your employment is exclusive with compensation of not less than US$12,000 paid by Philippine headquarters
3. visa is valid for 3 years or within your employment contract
4. visa will cover your spouse and unmarried children below 21 years of age

5. you are exempted from payment of immigration fees and alien registration fees, travel tax and importation of personal and household effects
6. you are exempted from securing ACR I-card and ECC.

Chapter IV

Taxation

Chapter IV
Taxation

Question: What are the rate of taxes for corporations?
Answer: Domestic corporation are subject on tax on net income inside and outside Philippines at the rate of 30%. The Minimum Corporate Income Tax (MCIT) on gross income, beginning on the 4th taxable year following the year the business operation started. The MCIT is imposed where the CIT at 30% is less than 2% MCIT on gross income.

A resident foreign corporation is taxed as a domestic corporation on income from Philippines.

Question: What is the new tax schedule for compensation income earners under the Tax Reform for Acceleration and Inclusion (TRAIN) RA No 10963?
Answer: Effective 1 January 2018, the compensation income earners will be taxed

Net taxable income		Tax rate
Over	But not over	
	250,000	0%
250,000	400,000	20% of excess over 250,000
400,000	800,000	30,000 + 25% excess over 400,000
800,000	2,000,000	130,000 + 30% of excess over 800,000
2,000,000	8,000,000	490,000 + 32% of excess over 2,000,000
8,000,000		2,410,000 + 35% of excess over 8,000,000

Note: BOI registered companies and PEZA registered companies enjoy tax incentives and privileges to promote foreign investment in the Philippines.

For further information, go to
https://www.bir.gov.ph/index.php/train.html

Chapter V

Board of Investment

Special Economic Zone Act of 1995

Philippine Investment Promotion Plan

Chapter V
Board of Investment under Executive Order No 226

The Board of Investment was created thru The Omnibus Investments Code of 1987 (EO 226) to promote, regulate and give incentives thru the Investments Priorities Plan (IPP) of especially identified economic investments of locals and foreign nationals.

Question: What business are qualified to register with BOI?
Answer: 1. Generally, the company must be a Philippine national and for partnerships and corporations at least 60% capital is owned by a Philippine national.

This limited 40% ownership for foreign nationals can be increased up to 100% foreign ownership in the following circumstances:

1. Business activity
 1.1. engaged in a pioneer project, the nature and capital requirements, processes, technical skills and relative business risks involved cannot be filled by a Philippine national; or
 1.2. at least 70% of total production is exported (may be reduced)
 1.3. will attain the status of a Philippine national within 30 years from registration or longer except business that export 100% total production.

2. You are proposing to engage in
2.1. preferred project listed in the current Investment Priority Plan (IPP)
2.2. if not listed, at least 50% of total production is for export or for existing producer it will export part of production or
2.3. sale abroad of export products brought by it from export producers or
2.4. render technical, professional or other services or
2.5. export television and motion pictures and musical recordings made or produced in the Philippines, directly or thru a registered trader; and

3. You are capable of operating on a sound and efficient basis contributing to the national development of the preferred area and the national economy

4. If you are engaged in business that is not preferred, you must install an accounting system that identifies the investments, revenues, costs and profits or losses the business.

Question: How are applications evaluated?
Answer: Your application will be evaluated under the following criteria:
1. extent of ownership and control by Philippine citizens
2. economic rates od return
3. measured capacity which is regularly reviewed
4. amount of foreign exchange earned in operation
5. extent of labour and local materials and resources used
6. extent which technologies are applied and adopted locally
7. amount of equity and ownership
8. other factors as determined by the Board of Investments.

Question: What are your rights as BOI registered business?
Answer: You are entitled to rights and guarantees provided in the Philippine Constitution and as a business owner you have the right of:
1. repatriation of investments
2. remittance of earnings
3. remittance of payment for foreign loans and contracts in relation to technological assistance contracts
4. freedom from expropriation except for public use with just compensation
5. no requisition of the property invested.

Question: What are the incentives to registered BOI business to less developed area (LDA)
Answer: The incentives are:

1. Pioneer incentives under its law of registration
2. Incentives for necessary and major infrastructure and public utilities.

Question: What are the tax incentives for BOI registered companies?

Answer: BOI registered companies enjoy the following tax benefits:
1. tax exemptions
2. tax credits
3. additional deductions from taxable income
4. zero-rated value added tax (VAT)
5. non-fiscal incentives

1. Tax exemptions

1.1. Income tax holiday (ITH)

1.1.1. BOI registered enterprises shall be exempt from the payment of income tax from the approved target or actual date of commercial operations, whichever comes first, but not earlier than the date of registration, as follows:

- 6 years for new projects granted pioneer status:
- 6 years for projects located in Less Developed Areas (LDAs), regardless of status (pioneer or non-pioneer) or type of projects (new or expansion)
- 4 years for new projects granted non-pioneer status; and
- 3 years for expansion and modernization projects

As a general rule, ITH shall be limited only to incremental sales given as specified base year.

1.1.2. Newly registered pioneer and non-pioneer enterprises, expansion enterprises granted pioneer incentives under Article 40 of EO 226, and those located in the LDA's may be granted 1 bonus year of ITH incentive for each of the following criterion:

- Capital equipment to labour ration criterion. The ration of derived dollar cost of capital equipment to the average number of direct labour does not exceed US$10,000; or
- Net foreign exchange earnings/savings criterion. The net foreign exchange savings or earnings for the first 3 years of commercial operation should at least be US$500,000; or
- Indigenous raw material cost criterion. The indigenous raw materials used in the manufacture or processing of the registered product is at least 50 % of the total cost of raw materials for each of the taxable year beginning the start of 8 Investment Incentives in the Philippines 2015 commercial operation up to when the extension using this criterion was applied for.

In no case shall a registered firm avail of ITH for a period exceeding 8 years.

1.2. Duty free importation of capital equipment, spare parts and accessories, subject to conditions.

A registered enterprise with a bonded manufacturing warehouse shall be exempt from customs duties and national internal revenue taxes on its importation of required supplies/spare parts for consigned equipment or those imported with incentives. This exemption shall not exceed 10 years from date of registration.

1.3. Exemption from wharfage dues and export tax, duty, impost and fees.

All enterprises registered under the IPP will be given a 10-year period from the date of registration to avail of the exemption from wharfage dues and any export, tax, impost and fees on its non-traditional export products.

1.4. Tax and duty-free importation of breeding stocks and genetic materials.

Agricultural production and processing projects will be exempt from the payment of all taxes and duties on their importation of breeding stocks and genetic materials within 10 years from the date of registration or commercial operations.

2. Tax credits

2.1. Tax credits on the purchase of domestic breeding stocks and genetic materials.

A tax credit equivalent to 100% of the value of national internal revenue taxes and customs duties that would have been waived (had these been imported) on the purchase of local breeding stocks and genetic materials within 10 years from the date of registration or commercial operations.

2.2. Tax credits on raw materials and supplies.

Tax credit equivalent to the national internal revenue taxes and duties paid on raw materials, supplies and semi-manufactured products use din the manufacture of export products and forming part thereof.

3. Additional deductions from taxable income

   3.1. Additional deduction for labour expense (ADLE).

   For the first 5 years from the date of registration, a registered enterprise shall be allowed an additional deduction from taxable income equivalent to 50% of the wages of additional skilled and unskilled workers in the direct labour force. This incentive shall be granted only of the enterprise meets a prescribed capital to labour ratio and shall not be availed of simultaneously with ITH. This additional deduction shall be doubled or become 100% if the activity is located in an LDA. The privilege, however, is not granted to mining and forestry-related projects as they would naturally be located in certain areas to be near their source of raw materials. ADLE cannot be simultaneously availed of with ITH.

   3.2. Additional deduction for necessary and major infrastructure work.

   A registered enterprise locating in LDAs or in areas deficient in infrastructure, public utilities, and other facilities may deduct from taxable income an amount equivalent to the expenses incurred in the development of necessary and major infrastructure works.

4. Zero-rated Value Added Tax (VAT)

The BOI endorses to the BIR two types of 0% VAT applications:

> 4.1. for purchased of raw material and supplies used in the manufacture and which form part of the registered export product; and

> 4.2. for purchases of goods, services, or properties of firms exporting 100% of their product. (Motor vehicles are not covered, except specialized vehicles such as backhoe, forklift, etc).

5. Non-fiscal incentives

> 5.1. Employment of foreign nationals in supervisory, technical or advisory positions for 5 years from registration extendible with the Board's discretion. The limitation period for the position of president, treasurer and general manager or equivalents do not apply if majority of capital stock is owned by foreign investors.

> 5.2. Simplified customs procedure for importation of equipment, spare parts, raw materials, and supplies and exports of processed products.

> 5.3. Importation of equipment for 10 years from date of registration

> 5.4. Operate a bonded manufacturing/trading warehouse subject to Customs rules and regulations.

The Special Economic Zone Act of 1995 (RA No 7916)

This law established special economic zones to encourage and promote particular areas for economic growth and development and created Philippine Economic Zone Authority (PEZA) to enforce the provisions of the Act.

Question: What are the activities eligible for PEZA registration and incentives?

Answer: Your company can engage in any of the following activities to avail of the benefits:

1. export manufacturing
2. information technology service export
3. tourism
4. medical tourism
5. agro-industrial export manufacturing
6. agro-industrial bio-fuel manufacturing
7. logistics and warehousing services
8. economic zone development operation
8.1. manufacturing economic zone development/operation
8.2. IT park development/operation
8.3. tourism economic zone development/operation
8.4. medical tourism economic zone development/operation
8.5. agro-industrial economic zone development/operation
8.6. retirement economic zone development operation
9. facilities providers
9.1. facilities for manufacturing enterprises
9.2. facilities for IT enterprises
9.3. retirement facilities
10. utilities

Question: What are the benefits of a PEZA-registered company within the special zones?

Answer: The benefits of PEZA- registered companies are:
1. all the tax benefits and incentives under EO 226

2. after the ITH period, you may avail of 5% preferential final tax of gross income instead of all national and local taxes
3. tax and duty-free importation of capital equipment, spare parts, raw materials and supplies
4. tax credit for exporters using local materials as inputs
5. deduction for expenses incurred for training skilled and unskilled labour, managerial or other management development programs.

Philippine investment Promotion Plan (PIPP)

These 19 agencies are tasked to promote and develop secure and special economic investment locations in the Philippines by granting tax incentives and cost effective labour supply, building infrastructures and business management.

1. Board of Investments
   For further information, go to http://boi.gov.ph/

2. Aurora Pacific Economic Zone and Freeport Area
   For further information, go to https://auroraecozone.com/

3. The Freeport Area of Bataan (FAB)
   For further information, go to http://afab.gov.ph/

4. Bases Conversion and Development Authority
   For further information, go to https://bcda.gov.ph/

5. Cagayan Economic Zone Authority
   For further information, go to https://ceza.gov.ph/

6. Clark Development Corporation
   For further information, go to https://www.clark.com.ph/

7. The Clark International Airport Corporation
   For further information, go to https://clarkinternationalairport.com/

8. The John Hay Management Corporation
   For further information, go to https://www.jhmc.com.ph/

9. The Mindanao Development Authority
   For further information, go to http://minda.gov.ph/

10. Philippine Economic Zone Authority
    For further information, go to   http://www.peza.gov.ph/

11. The Philippine Retirement Authority
    For further information, go to   https://pra.gov.ph/

12. The Phividec Industrial Authority
    For further information, go to   http://www.piamo.gov.ph/

13. Poro Point Management Corporation
    For further information, go to   http://www.poropointfreeport.gov.ph/

14. Regional Board of Investments – Autonomous Region of Muslim Mindanao
    For further information, go to   http://www.rboi.armm.gov.ph/

15. Subic Bay Metropolitan Authority
    For further information, go to   http://www.sbma.com/

16. Subic Clark Alliance for Development Council
    For further information, go to   http://scad.gov.ph/

17. Tourism Infrastructure and Enterprise Zone Authority
    For further information, go to   https://tieza.gov.ph/

18. Tourism Promotions Board
    For further information, go to   https://www.tpb.gov.ph/

19. Zamboanga City Special Economic Zone Authority
    For further information, go to   http://zfa.gov.ph/

Sources:

The Corporation Code of the Philippines (*Republic Act No* 11232)
Foreign Investments Act of 1991 (*Republic Act No* 70420)
Investment Incentives Act (*Republic Act No* 5186)
The Omnibus Investments Code of 1987 (*Executive Order No* 226)
The Special Economic Zone Act of 1995 (*Republic Act No* 7916 as amended by *Republic Act No* 8748)
11th Regular Foreign Investment Negative List as at 29 October 2019 (*Executive Order No* 65)
Philippine Retirement Authority (*Executive Order No* 1037 as amended by *Executive Order No* 26 as amended by *Republic Act No* 9593)
The Tax Reform for Acceleration and Inclusion (TRAIN) Act (*Republic Act No* 10963)
The Securities Act (*Commonwealth Act No* 83 as amended by the Revised Corporation Code (RCC) *Republic Act No* 11232)

About the Author

Michelle D Martinez is admitted to practice law in Australia and in the Philippines. She is a partner in Martinez Tria Lawyers, a boutique law firm in the City of Manila. Their law firm specialises in commercial and banking transactions including insolvency and bankruptcy, family law, criminal law, employment law and property and sales.

She is also a partner in Valera Burns Montero Tria and Associates located in Makati City which specialises in immigration law, mergers and acquisitions, financial and investment law, technology and data privacy law, intellectual property law and virtual and crypto currency laws.

Printed in Great Britain
by Amazon